Robert G. Ingersoll

Shakespeare

A lecture

Robert G. Ingersoll

Shakespeare
A lecture

ISBN/EAN: 9783337061876

Printed in Europe, USA, Canada, Australia, Japan

Cover: Foto ©ninafisch / pixelio.de

More available books at **www.hansebooks.com**

SHAKESPEARE.

A LECTURE

BY

ROBERT G. INGERSOLL.

Shakespeare. — An intellectual ocean, whose waves touched all the shores of thought.

NEW YORK.
C. P. FARRELL, PUBLISHER,
1895.

SHAKESPEARE.

I.

WILLIAM SHAKESPEARE was the greatest genius of our world. He left to us the richest legacy of all the dead—the treasures of the rarest soul that ever lived and loved and wrought of words the statues, pictures, robes and gems of thought. He was the greatest man that ever touched this grain of sand and tear. , we call the world.

It is hard to overstate the debt we owe to the men and women of genius. Take from our world what they have given, and all the niches would be empty, all the walls naked—meaning and connection would fall from words of poetry and fiction, music would go back to common air, and all the forms of subtle and enchanting Art would lose pro-

portion and become the unmeaning waste and shattered spoil of thoughtless Chance.

Shakespeare is too great a theme. I feel as
though endeavoring to grasp a globe so large that
the hand obtains no hold. He who would worthily
speak of the great dramatist should be inspired by
" a muse of fire that should ascend the brightest
heaven of invention " — he should have " a kingdom
for a stage, and monarchs to behold the swelling
scene."

More than three centuries ago, the most intellectual of the human race was born. He was not of
supernatural origin. At his birth there were no
celestial pyrotechnics. His father and mother were
both English, and both had the cheerful habit of
living in this world. The cradle in which he
was rocked was canopied by neither myth nor
miracle, and in his veins there was no drop of royal
blood.

This babe became the wonder of mankind.
Neither of his parents could read or write. He
grew up in a small and ignorant village on the banks
of the Avon, in the midst of the common people of
three hundred years ago. There was nothing in the
peaceful, quiet landscape on which he looked, noth-

ing in the low hills, the cultivated and undulating fields, and nothing in the murmuring stream, to excite the imagination — nothing, so far as we can see, calculated to sow the seeds of the subtlest and sublimest thought.

So there is nothing connected with his education, or his lack of education, that in any way accounts for what he did. It is supposed that he attended school in his native town — but of this we are not certain. Many have tried to show that he was, after all, of gentle blood, but the fact seems to be the other way. Some of his biographers have sought to do him honor by showing that he was patronized by Queen Elizabeth, but of this there is not the slightest proof.

As a matter of fact, there never sat on any throne, a king, queen, or emperor who could have honored William Shakespeare.

Ignorant people are apt to overrate the value of what is called education. The sons of the poor, having suffered the privations of poverty, think of wealth as the mother of joy. On the other hand, the children of the rich, finding that gold does not produce happiness, are apt to underrate the value of wealth. So the children of the educated often care but little for books, and hold all culture in contempt. The children of great authors do not, as a rule, become writers.

Nature is filled with tendencies and obstructions. Extremes beget limitations, even as a river by its own swiftness creates obstructions for itself.

Possibly, many generations of culture breed a desire for the rude joys of savagery, and possibly generations of ignorance breed such a longing for knowledge, that of this desire, of this hunger of the brain, Genius is born. It may be that the mind, by lying fallow, by remaining idle for generations, gathers strength.

Shakespeare's father seems to have been an ordinary man of his time and class. About the only thing we know of him is that he was officially reported for not coming monthly to church. This is good as far as it goes. We can hardly blame him, because at that time Richard Bifield was the minister at Stratford, and an extreme Puritan, one who read the Psalter by Sternhold and Hopkins.

The church was at one time Catholic, but in John Shakespeare's day it was Puritan, and in 1564, the year of Shakespeare's birth, they had the images defaced. It is greatly to the honor of John

Shakespeare that he refused to listen to the " tidings of great joy" as delivered by the Puritan Bifield.

Nothing is known of his mother, except her beautiful name — Mary Arden. In those days but little attention was given to the biographies of women. They were born, married, had children, and died. No matter how celebrated their sons became, the mothers were forgotten. In old times, when a man achieved distinction, great pains were taken to find out about the father and grandfather — the idea being that genius is inherited from the father's side. The truth is, that all great men have had great mothers. . Great women have had, as a rule, great fathers. The mother of Shakespeare was, without doubt, one of the greatest of women. She dowered her son with passion and imagination and the higher qualities of the soul, beyond all other men. It has been said that a man of genius should select his ancestors with great care—and yet there does not seem to be as much in heredity as most people think. The children of the great are often small. Pigmies are born in palaces, while over the children of genius is the roof of straw. Most of the great are like mountains, with the valley of ancestors on one side and the depression of posterity on the other.

In his day Shakespeare was of no particular importance. It may be that his mother had some marvelous and prophetic dreams, but Stratford was unconscious of the immortal child. He was never engaged in a reputable business. Socially he occupied a position below servants. The law described him as "a sturdy vagabond." He was neither a noble, a soldier, nor a priest. Among the half-civilized people of England, he who amused and instructed them was regarded as a menial. Kings had their clowns, the people their actors and musicians. Shakespeare was scheduled as a servant. It is thus that successful stupidity has always treated genius. Mozart was patronized by an Archbishop—lived in the palace,—but was compelled to eat with the scullions.

The composer of divine melodies was not fit to sit by the side of the theologian, who long ago would have been forgotten but for the fame of the composer.

We know but little of the personal peculiarities, of the daily life, or of what may be called the outward Shakespeare, and it may be fortunate that so little is

known. He might have been belittled by friendly
fools. What silly stories, what idiotic personal rem-
iniscences, would have been remembered by those
who scarcely saw him! We have his best—his
sublimest—and we have probably lost only the
trivial and the worthless. All that is known can be
written on a page.

We are tolerably certain of the date of his birth,
of his marriage and of his death. We think he went
to London in 1586, when he was twenty-two years
old. We think that three years afterwards he was
part owner of Blackfriars' Theatre. We have a few
signatures, some of which are supposed to be genuine. We know that he bought some land—that
he had two or three law-suits. We know the names
of his children. We also know that this incompar-
able man—so apart from, and so familiar with, all
the world—lived during his literary life in London—that he was an actor, dramatist and mana-
ger—that he returned to Stratford, the place of
his birth,—that he gave his writings to negli-
gence, deserted the children of his brain—that he
died on the anniversary of his birth at the age of
fifty-two, and that he was buried in the church
where the images had been defaced, and that on his

tomb was chiseled a rude, absurd and ignorant epitaph.

No letter of his to any human being has been found, and no line written by him can be shown.

And here let me give my explanation of the epitaph. Shakespeare was an actor —a disreputable business—but he made money—always reputable. He came back from London a rich man. He bought land, and built houses. Some of the supposed great probably treated him with deference. When he died he was buried in the church. Then came a reaction. The pious thought the church had been profaned. They did not feel that the ashes of an actor were fit to lie in holy ground. The people began to say the body ought to be removed. Then it was, as I believe, that Dr. John Hall, Shakespeare's son-in-law, had this epitaph cut on the tomb :

> "Good friend, for Jesus' sake forbeare
> To digg the dust enclosed heare :
> Blese be ye man yt spares thes stones,
> And curst be he yt moves my bones."

Certainly Shakespeare could have had no fear that his tomb would be violated. How could it have entered his mind to have put a warning, a threat and a blessing, upon his grave? But the ignorant people of that day were no doubt convinced that the epitaph was the voice of the dead, and so feeling they feared to invade the tomb. In this way the dust was left in peace.

This epitaph gave me great trouble for years. It puzzled me to explain why he, who erected the intellectual pyramids, — great ranges of mountains — should put such a pebble at his tomb. But when I stood beside the grave and read the ignorant words, the explanation I have given flashed upon me.

and the epitaph prevented his wife being buried beside him

IT has been said that Shakespeare was hardly mentioned by his contemporaries, and that he was substantially unknown. This is a mistake. In 1600 a book was published called " *England's Parnassus*," and it contained ninety extracts from Shakespeare. In the same year was published the " *Garden of the Muses*," containing several pieces from Shakespeare, Chapman, Marston and Ben Johnson. " *England's Helicon*" was printed in the same year, and contained poems from Spenser, Greene, Harvey and Shakespeare.

In 1600 a play was acted at Cambridge, in which

Shakespeare was alluded to as follows : " Why, here's
our fellow Shakespeare who puts them all down."
John Weaver published a book of poems in 1595, in
which there was a sonnet to Shakespeare. In
1598 Richard Bamfield wrote a poem to Shakespeare. Francis Meres, " clergyman, master of arts
in both universities, compiler of school books," was
the author of the " *Wits' Treasury.*" In this he
compares the ancient and modern tragic poets, and
mentions Marlowe, Peel, Kyd and Shakespeare.
So he compares the writers of comedies, and mentions Lilly, Lodge, Greene and Shakespeare. He
speaks of elegiac poets, and names Surrey, Wyatt,
Sidney, Raleigh and Shakespeare. He compares
the lyric poets, and names Spencer, Drayton,
Shakespeare and others. This same writer, speak-
ing of Horace, says that England has Sidney,
Shakespeare and others, and that "as the soul of
Euphorbus was thought to live in Pythagoras, so
the sweet-wittie soul of Ovid lives in the mellifluous
and honey-tongued Shakespeare." He also says :
" If the Muses could speak English, they would
speak in Shakespeare's phrase." This was in 1598.
In 1607, John Davies alludes in a poem to Shakespeare.

Of course we are all familiar with what rare Ben Jonson wrote. Henry Chettle took Shakespeare to task because he wrote nothing on the death of Queen Elizabeth.

It may be wonderful that he was not better known. But is it not wonderful that he gained the reputation that he did in so short a time, and that twelve years after he began to write he stood at least with the first?

III.

BUT there is a wonderful fact connected with the writings of Shakespeare: In the Plays there is no direct mention of any of his contemporaries. We do not know of any poet, author, soldier, sailor, statesman, priest, nobleman, king, or queen, that Shakespeare directly mentioned.

Is it not marvellous that he, living in an age of great deeds, of adventures in far off lands and un-known seas—in a time of religious wars—in the days of the Armada—the massacre of St. Bartholo-mew—the Edict of Nantes—the assassination of Henry III.—-the victory of Lepanto—the execution of Marie Stuart—did not mention the name of any

man or woman of his time? Some have insisted
that the paragraph ending with the lines :

" The imperial votress passed on in maiden meditation fancy
   free,"

referred to Queen Elizabeth ; but it is impossible
for me to believe that the daubed and wrinkled face,
the small black eyes, the cruel nose, the thin lips,
the bad ·teeth, and the red wig of Queen Elizabeth
could by any possibility have inspired these marvellous lines.

It is perfectly apparent from Shakespeare's writings that he knew but little of the nobility, little of
kings and queens. He gives to these supposed
great people great thoughts, and puts great words in
their mouths and makes them speak—not as they
really did—but as Shakespeare thought such people
should. This demonstrates that he did not know
them personally.

Some have insisted that Shakespeare mentions
Queen Elizabeth in the last Scene of Henry VIII.
The answer to this is that Shakespeare did not write
the last Scene in that Play. The probability is that
Fletcher was the author.

Shakespeare lived during the great awakening of

the world, when Europe emerged from the darkness of the Middle Ages, when the discovery of America had made England, that blossom of the Gulf-Stream, the centre of commerce, and during a period when some of the greatest writers, thinkers, soldiers and discoverers were produced.

Cervantes was born in 1547, dying on the same day that Shakespeare died. He was undoubtedly the greatest writer that Spain has produced. Rubens was born in 1577. Camoens, the Portuguese, the author of the *Lusiad*, died in 1597. Giordano Bruno—greatest of martyrs—was born in 1548—visited London in Shakespeare's time—delivered lectures at Oxford, and called that institution "the widow of learning." Drake circled the globe in 1580. Galileo was born in 1564—the same year with Shakespeare. Michael Angelo died in 1563. Kepler—he of the Three Laws—born in 1571. Calderon, the Spanish dramatist, born in 1601. Corneille, the French poet, in 1606. Rembrandt, greatest of painters, 1607. Shakespeare was born in 1564. In that year John Calvin died. What a glorious exchange!

Seventy-two years after the discovery of America Shakespeare was born, and England was filled with

the voyages and discoveries written by Hakluyt
and the wonders that had been seen by Raleigh, by
Drake, by Frobisher and Hawkins. London had
become the centre of the world, and representatives
from all known countries were in the new metropo-
lis. The world had been doubled. The imagination
had been touched and kindled by discovery. In the
far horizon were unknown lands, strange shores beyond untraversed seas. Toward every part of the
world were turned the prows of adventure. All
these things fanned the imagination into flame, and
this had its effect upon the literary and dramatic
world. And yet Shakespeare—the master spirit of
mankind—in the midst of these discoveries, of these
adventures, mentioned no navigator, no general, no
discoverer, no philosopher.

Galileo was reading the open volume of the sky
but Shakespeare did not mention him. This to me
is the most marvellous thing connected with this
most marvellous man.

At that time England was prosperous —was then
laying the foundation of her future greatness and
power.

When men are prosperous, they are in love with
life. Nature grows beautiful, the arts begin to

flourish, there is work for painter and sculptor, the poet is born, the stage is erected — and this life with which men are in love, is represented in a thousand forms.

Nature, or Fate, or Chance prepared a stage for Shakespeare, and Shakespeare prepared a stage for Nature.

Famine and faith go together. In disaster and want the gaze of man is fixed upon another world. He that eats a crust has a creed. Hunger falls upon its knees, and heaven, looked for through tears, is the mirage of misery. But prosperity brings joy and wealth and leisure — and the beautiful is born.

One of the effects of the world's awakening was Shakespeare. We account for this man as we do for the highest mountain, the greatest river, the most perfect gem. We can only say : He was.

> " It hath been taught us from the primal state
> That he which is was wished until he were."

IV.

IN Shakespeare's time the actor was a vagabond, the dramatist a disreputable person — and yet the greatest dramas were then written. In spite of law, and social ostracism, Shakespeare reared the many-colored dome that fills and glorifies the intellectual heavens.

Now the whole civilized world believes in the theatre — asks for some great dramatist — is hungry for a play worthy of the century, is anxious to give gold and fame to any one who can worthily put our age upon the stage — and yet no great play has been written since Shakespeare died.

Shakespeare pursued the highway of the right. He did not seek to put his characters in a position where it was right to do wrong. He was sound and healthy to the centre. It never occurred to him to write a play in which a wife's lover should be jealous of her husband.

There was in his blood the courage of his thought. He was true to himself and enjoyed the perfect freedom of the highest art. He did not write according to rules — but smaller men make rules from what he wrote.

How fortunate that Shakespeare was not educated at Oxford — that the winged god within him never knelt to the professor. How fortunate that this giant was not captured, tied and tethered by the literary Liliputians of his time.

He was an idealist. He did not — like most

writers of our time — take refuge in the real, hiding a lack of genius behind a pretended love of truth. All realities are not poetic, or dramatic, or even worth knowing. The real sustains the same relation to the ideal that a stone does to a statue — or that paint does to a painting. Realism degrades and impoverishes. In no event can a realist be more than an imitator and copyist. According to the realist's philosophy, the wax that receives and retains an image is an artist.

Shakespeare did not rely on the stage-carpenter, or the scenic painter. He put his scenery in his lines. There you will find mountains and rivers and seas, valleys and cliffs, violets and clouds, and over all " the firmament fretted with gold and fire." He cared little for plot, little for surprise. He did not rely on stage effects, or red fire. The plays grow before your eyes, and they come as the morning comes. Plot surprises but once. There must be something in a play besides surprise. Plot in an author is a kind of strategy — that is to say, a sort of cunning, and cunning does not belong to the highest natures.

There is in Shakespeare such a wealth of thought that the plot becomes almost immaterial — and such

is this wealth that you can hardly know the play —
there is too much.   After you have heard it again
and again, it seems as pathless as an untrodden
forest.

He belonged to all lands.   " Timon of Athens "
is as Greek as any tragedy of Eschylus.   " Julius
Cæsar " and " Coriolanus " are perfect Roman, and
as you read, the mighty ruins rise and the Eternal
City once again becomes the mistress of the world.
No play is more Egyptian than " Antony and Cleopatra "— the Nile runs through it, the shadows of
the pyramids fall upon it, and from its scenes the
Sphinx gazes forever on the outstretched sands.

" In " Lear " is the true pagan spirit.   " Romeo
and Juliet " is Italian — everything is sudden, love
bursts into immediate flower, and in every scene is
the climate of the land of poetry and passion.

The reason of this is, that Shakespeare dealt with
elemental things, with universal man.   He knew
that locality colors without changing, and that in all
surroundings the human heart is substantially the
same.

Not all the poetry written before his time would
make his sum — not all that has been written since,
added to all that was written before, would equal his.

There was nothing within the range of human thought, within the horizon of intellectual effort, that he did not touch. He knew the brain and heart of man — the theories, customs, superstitions, hopes, fears, hatreds, vices and virtues of the human race.

He knew the thrills and ecstacies of love, the savage joys of hatred and revenge. He heard the hiss of envy's snakes and watched the eagles of ambition soar. There was no hope that did not put its star above his head — no fear he had not felt — no joy that had not shed its sunshine on his face. He experienced the emotions of mankind. He was the intellectual spendthrift of the world. He gave with the generosity, the extravagance, of madness.

Read one play, and you are impressed with the idea that the wealth of the brain of a god has been exhausted — that there are no more comparisons, no more passions to be expressed, no more definitions, no more philosophy, beauty, or sublimity to be put in words — and yet, the next play opens as fresh as the dewy gates of another day.

The outstretched wings of his imagination filled the sky. He was the intellectual crown o' the earth.

V.

THE plays of Shakespeare show so much knowledge, thought and learning, that many people — those who imagine that universities furnish capacity — contend that Bacon must have been the author.

We know Bacon. We know that he was a scheming politician, a courtier, a time-server of church and king, and a corrupt judge. We know that he never admitted the truth of the Copernican system — that he was doubtful whether instruments were of any advantage in scientific investigation — that he was ignorant of the higher branches of mathematics, and that, as a matter of fact, he added but little to the knowledge of the world. When he was more than sixty years of age, he turned his attention to poetry, and dedicated his verses to George Herbert.

If you will read these verses you will say that the author of " Lear " and " Hamlet " did not write them.

Bacon dedicated his work on the *Advancement of Learning, Divine and Human*, to James I., and in his dedication he stated that there had not been, since the time of Christ, any king or monarch so learned in all erudition, divine or human. He placed James the First before Marcus Aurelius and

all other kings and emperors since Christ, and con-
cluded by saying that James the First had " the
power and fortune of a king, the illumination of a
priest, the learning and universality of a philosopher."
This was written of James the First, described by
Macauley as a " stammering, slobbering, trembling
coward, whose writings were deformed by the
grossest and vilest superstitions — witches being the
special objects of his fear, his hatred, and his perse-
cution."

It seems to have been taken for granted that if
Shakespeare was not the author of the great dramas,
Lord Bacon must have been.

It has been claimed that Bacon was the greatest
philosopher of his time. And yet in reading his
works we find that there was in his mind a strange
mingling of foolishness and philosophy. He takes
pains to tell us, and to write it down for the benefit
of posterity, that " snow is colder than water,
because it hath more spirit in it, and that quicksilver
is the coldest of all metals, because it is the fullest of
spirit."

He stated that he hardly believed that you could
contract air by putting opium on top of the weather
glass, and gave the following reason :

" I conceive that opium and the like make spirits fly rather by malignity than by cold."

This great philosopher gave the following recipe for staunching blood :

" Thrust the part that bleedeth into the body of a capon, new ripped and bleeding. This will staunch the blood. The blood, as it seemeth, sucking and drawing up by similitude of substance the blood it meeteth with, and so itself going back."

The philosopher also records this important fact :

" Divers witches among heathen and Christians have fed upon man's flesh to aid, as it seemeth, their imagination with high and foul vapors."

Lord Bacon was not only a philosopher, but he was a biologist, as appears from the following :

" As for living creatures, it is certain that their vital spirits are a substance compounded of an airy and flamy matter, and although air and flame being free will not mingle, yet bound in by a body that hath some fixing, will."

Now and then the inventor of deduction reasons by analogy. He **says** :

" As snow and ice holpen, and their cold activated by nitre or salt, will turn water into ice, so it may be it will turn wood or stiff clay into stone."

Bacon seems to have been a believer in the transmutation of metals, and solemnly gives a formula for changing silver or copper into gold. He also believed in the transmutation of plants, and had arrived at such a height in entomology that he informed the world that " insects have no blood."

It is claimed that he was a great observer, and as evidence of this he recorded the wonderful fact that " tobacco cut and dried by the fire loses weight ;" that " bears in the winter wax fat in sleep, though they eat nothing ;" that " tortoises have no bones ;" that " there is a kind of stone, if ground and put in water where cattle drink, the cows will give more milk ;" that " it is hard to cure a hurt in a Frenchman's head, but easy in his leg ; that it is hard to cure a hurt in an Englishman's leg, but easy in his head ;" that " wounds made with brass weapons are easier to cure than those made with iron;" that " lead will multiply and increase, as in statues buried in the ground ;" and that " the rainbow touching anything causeth a sweet smell."

Bacon seems also to have turned his attention to ornithology, and says that " eggs laid in the full of the moon breed better birds," and that " you can make swallows white by putting ointment on the eggs before they are hatched."

He also informs us " that witches cannot hurt kings
as easily as they can common people ;" that " per-
fumes dry and strengthen the brain ;" that " any one
in the moment of triumph can be injured by another
who casts an envious eye, and the injury is greatest
when the envious glance comes from the oblique
eye."

Lord Bacon also turned his attention to medicine,
and he states that " bracelets made of snakes are good
for curing cramps ;" that " the skin of a wolf might
cure the colic, because a wolf has great digestion ;"
that " eating the roasted brains of hens and hares
strengthens the memory ;" that " if a woman about
to become a mother eats a good many quinces and
considerable coriander seed, the child will be ingen-
ious," and that " the moss which groweth on the
skull of an unburied dead man is good for staunching blood."

He expresses doubt, however, " as to whether you
can cure a wound by putting ointment on the weapon
that caused the wound, instead of on the wound itself."

It is claimed by the advocates of the Baconian
theory that their hero stood at the top of science ;
and yet " it is absolutely certain that he was ignorant

" the law of the acceleration of falling bodies, although the law had been made known and printed
y Galileo thirty years before Bacon wrote upon the
ibject. Neither did this great man understand the
-inciple of the lever. He was not acquainted with
e precession of the equinoxes, and as a matter of
ct was ill-read in those branches of learning in
hich, in his time, the most rapid progress had been
ade."

After Kepler discovered his third law, which was on
e 15th of May, 1618, Bacon was more than ever
pposed to the Copernican system. This great man
as far behind his own time, not only in astronomy,
ut in mathematics. In the preface to the " De-
criptio Globi Intellectualis," it is admitted either
at Bacon had never heard of the correction of the
arallax, or was unable to understand it. He com-
lained on account of the want of some method for
hortening mathematical calculations ; and yet " Na-
ier's Logarithms " had been printed nine years be-
re the date of his complaint.

He attempted to form a table of specific gravities
y a rude process of his own, a process that no one
as ever followed ; and he did this in spite of the
act that a far better method existed.

We have the right to compare what Bacon wrote with what it is claimed Shakespeare produced. I call attention to one thing — to Bacon's opinion of human love. It is this :

" The stage is more beholding to love than the life of man. As to the stage, love is ever matter of comedies and now and then of tragedies, but in life it doth much mischief — sometimes like a siren, sometimes like a fury. Amongst all the great and worthy persons there is not one that hath been transported to the mad degree of love, which shows that great spirits and great business do keep out this weak passion."

The author of " Romeo and Juliet " never wrote that.

It seems certain that the author of the wondrous Plays was one of the noblest of men.

Let us see what sense of honor Bacon had.

In writing commentaries on certain passages of Scripture, Lord Bacon tells a courtier, who has committed some offense, how to get back into the graces of his prince or king. Among other things he tells him not to appear too cheerful, but to assume a very grave and modest face ; not to bring the matter up himself ; to be extremely industrious, so that the prince will see that it is hard to get along without him ; also to get his friends to tell the prince or king how badly he, the courtier, feels ; and then he says, all these failing, " let him contrive to transfer the fault to others."

It is true that we know but little of Shakespeare, and consequently do not positively know that he did not have the ability to write the Plays — but we do know Bacon, and we know that he could not have written these Plays — consequently, they must have been written by a comparatively unknown man — that is to say, by a man who was known by no other writings. The fact that we do not know Shakespeare, except through the Plays and Sonnets, makes it possible for us to believe that he was the author.

Some people have imagined that the Plays were written by several — but this only increases the wonder, and adds a useless burden to credulity.

Bacon published in his time all the writings that he claimed. Naturally, he would have claimed his best. Is it possible that Bacon left the wondrous children of his brain on the door-step of Shakespeare, and kept the deformed ones at home? Is it possible that he fathered the failures and deserted the perfect ?

Of course, it is wonderful that so little has been found touching Shakespeare — but is it not equally wonderful, if Bacon was the author, that not a line has been found in all his papers, containing a suggestion, or a hint, that he was the writer of these Plays? Is it not wonderful that no fragment of any scene — no line — no word — has been found?

Some have insisted that Bacon kept the authorship secret, because it was disgraceful to write Plays. This argument does not cover the Sonnets — and besides, one who had been stripped of the robes of office, for receiving bribes as a judge, could have borne the additional disgrace of having written "Hamlet." The fact that Bacon did not claim to be the author, demonstrates that he was not. Shakespeare claimed to be the author, and no one in his time or day denied the claim. This demonstrates that he was.

Bacon published his works, and said to the world : This is what I have done.

Suppose you found in a cemetery a monument erected to John Smith, inventor of the Smith-churn, and suppose you were told that Mr. Smith provided for the monument in his will, and dictated the inscription — would it be possible to convince you

that Mr. Smith was also the inventor of the locomo-
tive and telegraph?

Bacon's best can be compared with Shakespeare's
common, but Shakespeare's best rises above Bacon's
best, like a domed temple above a beggar's hut.

VI.

OF course it is admitted that there were many
dramatists before and during the time of
Shakespeare — but they were only the foot hills of
that mighty peak the top of which the clouds and
mists still hide. Chapman and Marlowe, Heywood
and Jonson, Webster, Beaumont and Fletcher wrote
some great lines, and in the monotony of declama-
tion now and then is found a strain of genuine music
— but all of them together constituted only a herald
of Shakespeare. In all these Plays there is but a
hint, a prophecy, of the great drama destined to revo-
lutionize the poetic thought of the world.

Shakespeare was the greatest of poets. What
Greece and Rome produced was great until his time.
" Lions make leopards tame."

The great poet is a great artist. He is painter
and sculptor. The greatest pictures and statues

have been painted and chiseled with words. They
outlast all others. All the galleries of the world are
poor and cheap compared with the statues and pictures in Shakespeare's book.

Language is made of pictures represented by
sounds. The outer world is a dictionary of the
mind, and the artist called the soul uses this dictionary of things to express what happens in the noise-
less and invisible world of thought. First a sound
represents something in the outer world, and afterwards something in the inner, and this sound at last
is represented by a mark, and this mark stands for a
picture, and every brain is a gallery, and the artists
—that is to say, the souls — exchange pictures and
statues.

All art is of the same parentage. The poet uses
words — makes pictures and statues of sounds. The
sculptor expresses harmony, proportion, passion, in
marble ; the composer, in music ; the painter in form
and color. The dramatist expresses himself not only
in words, not only paints these pictures, but he expresses his thought in action.

Shakespeare was not only a poet, but a dramatist,
and expressed the ideal, the poetic, not only in words,
but in action. There are the wit, the humor, the

pathos, the tragedy of situation, of relation. The
dramatist speaks and acts through others — his per-
sonality is lost. The poet lives in the world of
thought and feeling, and to this the dramatist adds
the world of action. He creates characters that
seem to act in accordance with their own natures
and independently of him. He compresses lives into
hours, tells us the secrets of the heart, shows us the
springs of action — how desire bribes the judgment
and corrupts the will — how weak the reason is
when passion pleads, and how grand it is to stand
for right against the world.

It is not enough to say fine things, — great things,
dramatic things, must be done.

Let me give you an illustration of dramatic inci-
dent accompanying the highest form of poetic expression :

Macbeth having returned from the murder of
Duncan says to his wife :

> "Methought I heard a voice cry : Sleep no more,
>   Macbeth does murder sleep ; the innocent sleep ;
>   Sleep, that knits up the ravelled sleeve of care,
>   The death of each day's life, sore labor's bath,
>   Balm of hurt minds, great Nature's second course,
>   Chief nourisher in life's feast."   *   *   *

"Still it cried : Sleep no more, to all the house,
  Glamis hath murdered sleep, and therefore Cawdor
  Shall sleep no more—Macbeth shall sleep no more."

She exclaims :

"Who was it that thus cried?
  Why, worthy Thane, you do unbend your noble strength
  To think so brain-sickly of things ; get some water,
  And wash this filthy witness from your hand.
  Why did you bring the daggers from the place?"

Macbeth was so overcome with horror at his own deed, that he not only mistook his thoughts for the words of others, but was so carried away and beyond himself that he brought with him the daggers — the evidence of his guilt — the daggers that he should have left with the dead.   This is dramatic.

In the same play, the difference of feeling before and after the commission of a crime is illustrated to perfection.   When Macbeth is on his way to assassinate the king, the bell strikes, and he says, or whispers :

"Hear it not, Duncan, for it is a knell."

Afterward, when the deed has been committed, and a knocking is heard at the gate, he cries :

"Wake Duncan with thy knocking. I would thou couldst."

Let me give one more instance of dramatic action. When Antony speaks above the body of Cæsar he says :

> " You all do know this mantle : I remember
> The first time ever Cæsar put it on —
> 'Twas on a summer's evening, in his tent,
> That day he overcame the Nervii :
> Look ! In this place ran Cassius' dagger through :
> See what a rent the envious Casca made !
> Through this the well-beloved Brutus stabbed,
> And as he plucked his cursed steel away,
> Mark how the blood of Cæsar followed it."

VII.

THERE are men, and many of them, who are always trying to show that somebody else chiseled the statue or painted the picture, — that the poem is attributed to the wrong man, and that the battle was really won by a subordinate.

Of course Shakespeare made use of the work of others — and, we might almost say, of all others. Every writer must use the work of others. The only question is, how the accomplishments of other minds are used, whether as a foundation to build higher, or whether stolen to the end that the thief may make a reputation for himself, without adding to the great structure of literature.

Thousands of people have stolen stones from the Coliseum to make huts for themselves. So thousands of writers have taken the thoughts of others with which to adorn themselves. These are plagiarists. But the man who takes the thought of another, adds to it, gives it intensity and poetic form, throb and life, — is in the highest sense original.

Shakespeare found nearly all of his facts in the writings of others and was indebted to others for most of the stories of his plays. The question is not: Who furnished the stone, or who owned the quarry, but who chiseled the statue ?

We now know all the books that Shakespeare could have read, and consequently know many of the sources of his information. We find in *Pliny's Natural History*, published in 1601, the following : " The sea Pontis evermore floweth and runneth out into the Propontis ; but the sea never retireth back again with the Impontis." This was the raw material, and out of it Shakespeare made the following :

> "Like to the Pontic Sea,
>   Whose icy current and compulsive course
>   Ne'er feels retiring ebb, but keeps due on

To the Propontic and the Hellespont——
Even so my bloody thoughts, with violent pace,
Shall ne'er turn back, ne'er ebb to humble love,
Till that a capable and wide revenge
Swallow them up." ·

Perhaps we can give an idea of the difference between Shakespeare and other poets, by a passage from " Lear."   When Cordelia places her hand upon her father's head and speaks of the night and of the storm, an ordinary poet might have said :

"On such a night, a dog
  Should have stood against my fire."

A very great poet might have gone a step further and exclaimed :

" On such a night, mine enemy's dog
  Should have stood against my fire."

But Shakespeare said :   .

" Mine enemy's dog, though he had bit me,
  Should have stood, that night, against my fire."

Of all the poets — of all the writers — Shakespeare is the most original.   He is as original as Nature.
It may truthfully be said that " Nature wants stuff to vie strange forms with fancy, to make another."

VIII.

THERE is in the greatest poetry a kind of extravagance that touches the infinite, and in this
Shakespeare exceeds all others.

You will remember the description given of the
voyage of Paris in search of Helen :

" The seas and winds, old wranglers, made a truce,
    And did him service ; he touched the ports desired,
    And for an old aunt, whom the Greeks held captive,
    He brought a Grecian queen whose youth and freshness
    Wrinkles Apollo, and makes stale the morning."

So, in Pericles, when the father finds his daughter,
he cries out :

    " O Helicanus ! strike me, honored sir ;
        Give me a gash, put me to present pain,
        Lest this great sea of joys, rushing upon me,
        O'erbear the shores of my mortality."

The greatest compliment that man has ever paid
to the woman he adores is this line :

    " Eyes that do mislead the morn."

Nothing can be conceived more perfectly poetic.

In that marvellous play, the " Midsummer Night's
Dream," is one of the most extravagant things in
literature :

" Thou rememberest
　　Since once I sat upon a promontory,
　　And heard a mermaid on a dolphin's back
　　Uttering such dulcet and harmonious breath
　　That the rude sea grew civil at her song,
　　And certain stars shot madly from their spheres
　　To hear the sea-maid's music."

This is so marvellously told that it almost seems
probable.

So the description of Mark Antony :

　　　　" For his bounty
　　There was no winter in't — an autumn t'was
　　That grew the more by reaping.. His delights
　　Were dolphin-like—they showed his back above
　　The element they lived in."

Think of the astronomical scope and amplitude of
this :

　　" Her bed is India—there she lies a pearl."

Is there anything more intense than these words
of Cleopatra ?

　　" Rather on Nilus mud lay me stark naked
　　And let the water-flies blow me into abhorring."

Or this of Isabella :

" The impression of keen whips I'd wear as rubies,
　　And strip myself to death as to a bed
　　That longing I've been sick for, ere I yield
　　My body up to shame."

Is there an intellectual man in the world who will not agree with this?

> " Let me not live
>   After my flame lacks oil, to be the snuff
>   Of younger spirits."

Can anything exceed the words of Troilus when parting with Cressida :

> " We two, that with so many thousand sighs
>   Did buy each other, most poorly sell ourselves
>   With the rude brevity and discharge of one.
>   Injurious time now with a robber's haste
>   Crams his rich thievery up, he knows not how ;
>   As many farewells as be stars in heaven,
>   With distinct breath and consigned kisses to them,
>   He fumbles up into a loose adieu,
>   And scants us with a single famished kiss,
>   Distasted with the salt of broken tears."

Take this example, where pathos almost touches the grotesque.

> " O dear Juliet, why art thou yet so fair ?
>   Shall I believe that unsubstantial death is amorous,
>   And that the lean, abhorred monster keeps thee here
>   I' the dark, to be his paramour?"

Often when reading the marvellous lines of Shake-speare, I feel that his thoughts are " too subtle potent, tuned too sharp in sweetness, for the capacity of my

ruder powers." Sometimes I cry out, " O churl! —
write all, and leave no thoughts for those who follow
after."

IX.

SHAKESPEARE was an innovator, an iconoclast.
He cared nothing for the authority of men or
of schools. He violated the "unities," and cared
nothing for the models of the ancient world.

The Greeks insisted that nothing should be in a
play that did not tend to the catastrophe. They did
not believe in the episode — in the sudden contrasts
of light and shade — in mingling the comic and the
tragic. The sunlight never fell upon their tears, and
darkness did not overtake their laughter. They believed that nature sympathized or was in harmony
with the events of the play. When crime was about
to be committed — some horror to be perpetrated —
the light grew dim, the wind sighed, the trees shiv-
ered, and upon all was the shadow of the coming
event.

Shakespeare knew that the play had little to do
with the tides and currents of universal life — that
Nature cares neither for smiles nor tears, for life nor

death, and that the sun shines as gladly on coffins as on cradles.

The first time I visited the Place de la Concorde, where during the French Revolution stood the guillotine, and where now stands an Egyptian obelisk — a bird, sitting on the top, was singing with all its might. — Nature forgets.

One of the most notable instances of the violation by Shakespeare of the classic model, is found in the 6th Scene of the I. Act of Macbeth.

When the King and Banquo approach the castle in which the King is to be murdered that night, no shadow falls athwart the threshold. So beautiful is the scene that the King says :

> "This castle hath a pleasant seat ; the air
> Nimbly and sweetly recommends itself
> Unto our gentle senses."

And Banquo adds :

> "This guest of summer,
> The temple-haunting martlet, does approve
> By his loved mansionry that the heaven's breath
> Smells wooingly here ; no jutty, frieze,
> Buttress, nor coign of vantage, but this bird
> Hath made his pendent bed and procreant cradle.
> Where they most breed and haunt, I have observed
> The air is delicate."

Another notable instance is the porter scene immediately following the murder. So, too, the dialogue with the clown who brings the asp to Cleopatra just before the suicide, illustrates my meaning.

I know of one paragraph in the Greek drama worthy of Shakespeare. This is in " Medea." When Medea kills her children she curses Jason, using the ordinary Billingsgate and papal curse, but at the conclusion says : " I pray the gods to make him virtuous, that he may the more deeply feel the pang that I inflict."

Shakespeare dealt in lights and shadows. He was intense. He put noons and midnights side by side. No other dramatist would have dreamed of adding to the pathos — of increasing our appreciation of Lear's agony, by supplementing the wail of the mad king with the mocking laughter of a loving clown.

X.

THE ordinary dramatists — the men of talent — (and there is the same difference between talent and genius that there is between a stone-mason and a sculptor) create characters that become types. Types are of necessity caricatures — actual men and women are to some extent contradictory in their actions. Types are blown in the one direction by the one wind—characters have pilots.

In real people, good and evil mingle. Types are all one way, or all the other—all good, or all bad, all wise or all foolish.

Pecksniff was a perfect type, a perfect hypocrite—and will remain a type as long as language lives—a hypocrite that even drunkenness could not change. Everybody understands Pecksniff, and compared with him Tartuffe was an honest man.

Hamlet is an individual, a person, an actual being—and for that reason there is a difference of opinion as to his motives and as to his character. We differ about Hamlet as we do about Cæsar, or about Shakespeare himself.

Hamlet saw the ghost of his father and heard again his father's voice, and yet, afterwards, he speaks of "the undiscovered country from whose bourne no traveller returns."

In this there is no contradiction. The reason outweighs the senses. If we should see a dead man rise from his grave, we would not, the next day, believe that we did. No one can credit a miracle until it becomes so common that it ceases to be miraculous.

Types are puppets — controlled from without — characters act from within. There is the same difference between characters and types that there is between springs and water-works, between canals and rivers, between wooden soldiers and heroes.

In most plays and in most novels the characters are so shadowy that we have to piece them out with the imagination.

One waking in the morning sometimes sees at the foot of his bed a strange figure — it may be of an ancient lady with cap and ruffles and with the expression of garrulous and fussy old age — but when the light gets stronger, the figure gradually changes and he sees a few clothes on a chair.

The dramatist lives the lives of others, and in order to delineate character must not only have imagination but sympathy with the character delineated. The great dramatist thinks of a character as an entirety, as an individual.

I once had a dream, and in this dream I was discussing a subject with another man. It occurred to me that I was dreaming, and I then said to myself: If this is a dream, I am doing the talking for both sides — consequently I ought to know in advance what the other man is going to say. In my dream I tried the experiment. I then asked the other man a question, and before he answered made up my mind what the answer was to be. To my surprise, the man did not say what I expected he would, and so great was my astonishment that I awoke.

It then occurred to me that I had discovered the secret of Shakespeare. He did, when awake, what I did when asleep — that is, he threw off a character so perfect that it acted independently of him.

In the delineation of character Shakespeare has no rivals. He creates no monsters. His characters do not act without reason, without motive.

Iago had his reasons. In Caliban, nature was not destroyed—and Lady Macbeth certifies that the woman still was in her heart, by saying :

"Had he not resembled my father as he slept, I had done it."

Shakespeare's characters act from within. They are centres of energy. They are not pushed by unseen hands, or pulled by unseen strings. They have objects, desires. They are persons—real, living beings.

Few dramatists succeed in getting their characters loose from the canvas—their backs stick to the wall —they do not have free and independent action—

they have no background, no unexpressed motives —no untold desires. They lack the complexity of the real.

Shakespeare makes the character true to itself. Christopher Sly, surrounded by the luxuries of a lord, true to his station, calls for a pot of the smallest ale.

Take one expression by Lady Macbeth. You remember that after the murder is discovered—after the alarm bell is rung—she appears upon the scene wanting to know what has happened. Macduff refuses to tell her, saying that the slightest word would murder as it fell. At this moment Banquo comes upon the scene and Macduff cries out to him :

"Our royal master's murdered."

What does Lady Macbeth then say? She in fact makes a confession of guilt. The weak point in the terrible tragedy is that Duncan was murdered in Macbeth's castle. So when Lady Macbeth hears what they suppose is news to her, she cries:

"What! In our house !"

Had she been innocent, her horror of the crime would have made her forget the place—the venue. Banquo sees through this, and sees through her.

Her expression was a light, by which he saw her
guilt—and he answers :

"Too cruel anywhere."

No matter whether Shakespeare delineated clown
or king, warrior or maiden—no matter whether his
characters are taken from the gutter or the throne—
each is a work of consummate art, and when he is
unnatural, he is so splendid that the defect is forgotten.

When Romeo is told of the death of Juliet, and
thereupon makes up his mind to die upon her grave,
he gives a description of the shop where poison
could be purchased. He goes into particulars and
tells of the alligators stuffed, of the skins of ill-shaped
fishes, of the beggarly account of empty boxes, of
the remnants of pack-thread, and old cakes of roses
—and while it is hardly possible to believe that
under such circumstances a man would take the
trouble to make an inventory of a strange kind of
drug-store, yet the inventory is so perfect—the
picture is so marvellously drawn—that we forget to
think whether it is natural or not.

In making the frame of a great picture—of a great
scene—Shakespeare was often careless, but the

picture is perfect. In making the sides of the arch he was negligent, but when he placed the keystone, it burst into blossom..// Of course there are many lines in Shakepeare that never should have been written. In other words, there are imperfections in his plays. But we must remember that Shakespeare furnished the torch that enables us to see these imperfections.

Shakespeare speaks through his characters, and we must not mistake what the characters say, for the opinion of Shakespeare. No one can believe that Shakespeare regarded life as "a tale told by an idiot, full of sound and fury, signifying nothing." That was the opinion of a murderer, surrounded by avengers, and whose wife — partner in his crimes — troubled with thick-coming fancies — had gone down to her death.

Most actors and writers seem to suppose that the lines called " The Seven Ages " contain Shakespeare's view of human life. Nothing could be farther from the truth. The lines were uttered by a cynic, in contempt and scorn of the human race.

Shakespeare did not put his characters in the livery and uniform of some weakness, peculiarity or passion. He did not use names as tags or brands. He

did not write under the picture, " This is a villain."
His characters need no suggestive names to tell us
what they are — we see them and we know them for
ourselves.

It may be that in the greatest utterances of the
greatest characters in the supreme moments, we
have the real thoughts, opinions and convictions of
Shakespeare.

Of all writers Shakespeare is the most impersonal.
He speaks through others, and the others seem to
speak for themselves. The didactic is lost in the
dramatic. He does not use the stage as a pul-
pit to enforce some maxim. He is as reticent as
Nature.

He idealizes the common and transfigures all
he touches—but he does not preach. He was in-
terested in men and things as they were. He did
not seek to change them — but to portray. He was
Nature's mirror—and in that mirror Nature saw
herself.

When I stood amid the great trees of Cali-
fornia that lift their spreading capitals against
the clouds, looking like Nature's columns to
support the sky, I thought of the poetry of Shakespeare.

XI.

WHAT a procession of men and women — states-
men and warriors — kings and clowns —
issued from Shakespeare's brain. What women !

Isabella—in whose spotless life love and reason
blended into perfect truth.

Juliet—within whose heart passion and purity
met like white and red within the bosom of a rose.

Cordelia—who chose to suffer loss, rather than
show her wealth of love with those who gilded lies
in hope of gain.

Hermione— "tender as infancy and grace"—who
bore with perfect hope and faith the cross of shame,
and who at last forgave with all her heart.

Desdemona—so innocent, so perfect, her love so
pure, that she was incapable of suspecting that another could suspect, and who with dying words
sought to hide her lover's crime—and with her last
faint breath uttered a loving lie that burst into a
perfumed lily between her pallid lips.

Perdita—A violet dim, and sweeter than the lids
of Juno's eyes—"The sweetest low-born lass that
ever ran on the green sward."   And

Helena—who said :

" I know I love in vain, strive against hope —
   Yet in this captious and intenable sieve
   I still pour in the waters of my love,
   And lack not to lose still.
   Thus, Indian-like,
   Religious in mine error, I adore
   The sun that looks upon his worshipper,
   But knows of him no more."

Miranda — who told her love as gladly as a flower gives its bosom to the kisses of the sun.

And *Cordelia*, whose kisses cured and whose tears restored. And stainless *Imogen*, who cried : " What is it to be false ? "

And here is the description of the perfect woman :

" To feed for aye her lamp and flames of love ;
   To keep her constancy in plight and youth —
   Outliving beauty's outward with a mind
   That doth renew swifter than blood decays. "

Shakespeare has done more for woman than all the other dramatists of the world.

For my part. I love the Clowns. I love *Launce* and his dog Crabb, and *Gobbo*, whose conscience threw its arms around the neck of his heart, and *Touchstone*, with his lie seven times removed ; and dear old *Dogberry* — a pretty piece of flesh, tedious as a king. And *Bottom*, the very paramour for a

sweet voice, longing to take the part to tear a cat in ;
and *Autolycus*, the snapper-up of unconsidered trifles,
sleeping out the thought for the life to come. And
great *Sir John*, without conscience, and for that
reason unblamed and enjoyed — and who at the end
babbles of green fields, and is almost loved. And
ancient *Pistol*, the world his oyster. And *Bardolph*,
with the flea on his blazing nose, putting beholders
in mind of a damned soul in hell. And the poor
Fool, who followed the mad king, and went " to bed
at noon." And the clown who carried the worm of
Nilus, whose " biting was immortal." And *Corin*,
the shepherd — who described the perfect man : " I
am a true laborer : I earn that I eat — get that I
wear — owe no man aught — envy no man's happiness — glad of other men's good — content."

And mingling in this motley throng, *Lear*, within
whose brain a tempest raged until the depths were
stirred, and the intellectual wealth of a life was given
back to memory — and then by madness thrown to
storm and night — and when I read the living lines
I feel as though I looked upon the sea and saw it
wrought by frenzied whirlwinds, until the buried
treasures and the sunken wrecks of all the years
were cast upon the shores.

And *Othello* — who like the base Indian threw a pearl away richer than all his tribe.

And *Hamlet* — thought-entangled — hesitating between two worlds.

And *Macbeth* — strange mingling of cruelty and conscience, reaping the sure harvest of successful crime — " Curses not loud but deep — mouth-honor — breath."

And *Brutus*, falling on his sword that Cæsar might be still.

And *Romeo*, dreaming of the white wonder of Juliet's hand. And *Ferdinand*, the patient log-man for Miranda's sake. And *Florizel*, who, " for all the sun sees, or the close earth wombs, or the profound seas hide," would not be faithless to the low-born lass. And *Constance*, weeping for her son, while grief " stuffs out his vacant garments with his form."

And in the midst of tragedies and tears, of love and laughter and crime, we hear the voice of the good friar, who declares that in every human heart, as in the smallest flower, there are encamped the opposed hosts of good and evil — and our philosophy is interrupted by the garrulous old nurse, whose talk is as busily useless as the babble of a stream that hurries by a ruined mill.

From every side the characters crowd upon us — the men and women born of Shakespeare's brain. They utter with a thousand voices the thoughts of the " myriad-minded " man, and impress themselves upon us as deeply and vividly as though they really lived with us.

Shakespeare alone has delineated love in every possible phase—has ascended to the very top, and actually reached heights that no other has imagined. I do not believe the human mind will ever produce or be in a position to appreciate, a greater love-play than " Romeo and Juliet." It is a symphony in which all music seems to blend. The heart bursts into blossom, and he who reads feels the swooning intoxication of a divine perfume.

In the alembic of Shakespeare's brain the baser metals were turned to gold—passions became virtues—weeds became exotics from some diviner land—and common mortals made of ordinary clay outranked the Olympian Gods. In his brain there was the touch of chaos that suggests the infinite— that belongs to genius. Talent is measured and mathematical—dominated by prudence and the thought of use. Genius is tropical. The creative instinct runs riot, delights in extravagance and waste, and overwhelms the mental beggars of the world with uncounted gold and unnumbered gems.

Some things are immortal : The plays of Shakespeare, the marbles of the Greeks, and the music of Wagner.

XII.

SHAKESPEARE was the greatest of philosophers. He knew the conditions of success — of happiness — the relations that men sustain to each other, and the duties of all. He knew the tides and currents of the heart — the cliffs and caverns of the brain. He knew the weakness of the will, the sophistry of desire — and

"That pleasure and revenge have ears more deaf than adders to the voice of any true decision."

He knew that the soul lives in an invisible world — that flesh is but a mask, and that

"There is no art to find the mind's construction
In the face."

He knew that courage should be the servant of judgment, and that

> " When valor preys on reason it eats the sword
>   It fights with."

He knew that man is never master of the event, that he is to some extent the sport or prey of the blind forces of the world, and that

> " In the reproof of chance lies the true proof of men."

Feeling that the past is unchangeable, and that that which must happen is as much beyond control as though it had happened, he says :

> " Let determined things to destiny
>   Hold unbewailed their way."

Shakespeare was great enough to know that every human being prefers happiness to misery, and that crimes are but mistakes. Looking in pity upon the human race, upon the pain and poverty, the crimes and cruelties, the limping travelers on the thorny paths, he was great and good enough to say :

> " There is no darkness but ignorance."

In all the philosophies there is no greater line. This great truth fills the heart with pity.

He knew that place and power do not give happiness — that the crowned are subject as the lowest to fate and chance.

> " Within the hollow crown
> That rounds the mortal temples of a king
> Keeps death his Court, and there the antic sits
> Scoffing his state and grinning at his pomp,
> Allowing him a brief and little scene
> To monarchize by fear and kill with looks,
> Infusing him with self and vain conceit—
> As if this flesh that walls about our life
> Were brass impregnable ; and humored thus,
> Comes at the last and with a little pin
> Bores through his castle wall—and farewell king!''

So, too, he knew that gold could not bring joy —
that death and misfortune come alike to rich and
poor, because :

> " If thou art rich thou art poor ;
> For like an ass whose back with ingots bows
> Thou bearest thy heavy riches but a journey,
> And death unloads thee."

In some of his philosophy there was a kind of
scorn — a hidden meaning that could not in his day
and time have safely been expressed. You will
remember that Laertes was about to kill the king,
and this king was the murderer of his own brother,
and sat upon the throne by reason of his crime —
and in the mouth of such a king Shakespeare puts
these words :

> " There's such divinity doth hedge a king."

So, in Macbeth :

"How he solicits Heaven himself best knows ; but
    strangely visited people
All swollen and ulcerous, pitiful to the eye,
The mere despairs of surgery, he cures ;
Hanging a golden stamp about their necks.
Put on with holy prayers ; and 'tis spoken
To the succeeding royalty — he leaves
The healing benediction.   With this strange virtue
He hath a heavenly gift of prophecy,
And sundry blessings hang about his throne,
That speak him full of grace."

Shakespeare was the master of the human heart —
knew all the hopes, fears, ambitions, and passions
that sway the mind of man ; and thus knowing, he
declared that

"Love is not love that alters
When it alteration finds."

This is the sublimest declaration in the literature
of the world.

Shakespeare seems to give the generalization —
the result — without the process of thought. He
seems always to be at the conclusion — standing
where all truths meet.

In one of the Sonnets is this fragment of a line
that contains the highest possible truth :

"Conscience is born of love."

If man were incapable of suffering, the words right and wrong never could have been spoken. If man were destitute of imagination, the flower of pity never could have blossomed in his heart.

We suffer—we cause others to suffer—those that we love—and of this fact conscience is born.

Love is the many-colored flame that makes the fireside of the heart. It is the mingled spring and autumn—the perfect climate of the soul.

XIII.

IN the realm of comparison Shakespeare seems to have exhausted the relations, parallels and similitudes of things. He only could have said :

"Tedious as a twice-told tale
Vexing the ears of a drowsy man."

"Duller than a great thaw.
Dry as the remainder biscuit after a voyage."

In the words of Ulysses, spoken to Achilles, we find the most wonderful collection of pictures and comparisons ever compressed within the same number of lines :

" Time hath, my lord, a wallet at his back,
Wherein he puts alms for oblivion,—
A great-sized monster of ingratitudes—
Those scraps are good deeds passed ; which are devoured
As fast as they are made, forgot as soon
As done ; perseverance, dear my lord,
Keeps honor bright : to have done is to hang
Quite out of fashion, like a rusty mail
In monumental mockery.   Take the instant way ;
For honor travels in a strait so narrow
Where one but goes abreast ; keep then the path ;
For emulation hath a thousand sons
That one by one pursue ; if you give way,
Or hedge aside from the direct forthright,
Like to an entered tide, they all rush by
And leave you hindmost :
Or, like a gallant horse fallen in first rank,
Lie there for pavement to the abject rear,
O'errun and trampled on : then what they do in present,
Tho' less than yours in past, must o'ertop yours ;
For time is like a fashionable host
That slightly shakes his parting guest by the hand,
And with his arms outstretched as he would fly,
Grasps in the comer : Welcome ever smiles,
And Farewell goes out sighing."

So the words of Cleopatra, when Charmain
speaks :

" Peace, peace :
Dost thou not see my baby at my breast
That sucks the nurse asleep ? "

XIV.

NOTHING is more difficult than a definition — a crystallization of thought so perfect that it emits light. Shakespeare says of suicide :

> "It is great to do that thing
> That ends all other deeds,
> Which shackles accident, and bolts up change."

He defines drama to be :

> "Turning the accomplishments of many years
> Into an hour glass."

Of death :

> "This sensible warm motion to become a kneaded clod,
> To lie in cold obstruction and to rot."

Of memory :

> "The warder of the brain."

Of the body :

> "This muddy vesture of decay."

And he declares that

> "Our little life is rounded with a sleep."

He speaks of Echo as :

> "The babbling gossip of the air" —

Romeo, addressing the poison that he is about to take, says :

"Come, bitter conduct, come unsavory guide,
Thou desperate pilot, now at once run on
The dashing rocks thy sea-sick, weary bark."

He describes the world as

"This bank and shoal of time."

He says of rumor —

"That it doubles, like the voice and echo."

It would take days to call attention to the perfect
definitions, comparisons and generalizations of
Shakespeare. He gave us the deeper meanings of
our words — taught us the art of speech. He was
the lord of language — master of expression and
compression.

He put the greatest thoughts into the shortest
words — made the poor rich and the common royal.

Production enriched his brain. Nothing exhausted
him. The moment his attention was called to any
subject — comparisons, definitions, metaphors and
generalizations filled his mind and begged for utter-
ance. His thoughts like bees robbed every blossom
in the world, and then with "merry march" brought
the rich booty home "to the tent royal of their
emperor."

Shakespeare was the confidant of Nature. To
him she opened her "infinite book of secrecy," and
in his brain were "the hatch and brood of time."

XV.

THERE is in Shakespeare the mingling of laughter and tears, humor and pathos. Humor is the rose, wit the thorn. Wit is a crystallization, humor an efflorescence. Wit comes from the brain, humor from the heart. Wit is the lightning of the soul.

In Shakespeare's nature was the climate of humor. He saw and felt the sunny side even of the saddest things. " You have seen sunshine and rain at once." So Shakespeare's tears fell oft upon his smiles. In moments of peril — on the very darkness of death - there comes a touch of humor that falls like a fleck of sunshine.

Gonzalo, when the ship is about to sink, having seen the boatswain, exclaims :

"I have great comfort from this fellow ;
    Methinks he hath no drowning mark upon him ;
    His complexion is perfect gallows. "

Shakespeare is filled with the strange contrasts of grief and laughter. While poor Hero is supposed to be dead — wrapped in the shroud of dishonor — Dogberry and Verges unconsciously put again the wedding wreath upon her pure brow.

The soliloquy of Launcelot — great as Hamlet's — offsets the bitter and burning words of Shylock.

There is only time to speak of Maria in " Twelfth Night," of Autolycus in the " Winter's Tale," of the parallel drawn by Fluellen between Alexander of Macedon and Harry of Monmouth, or of the mar- vellous humor of Falstaff, who never had the faintest thought of right or wrong — or of Mercutio, that embodiment of wit and humor — or of the grave- diggers who lamented that "great folk should have countenance in this world to drown and hang them- selves, more than their even Christian," and who reached the generalization that " the gallows does well because it does well to those who do ill."

There is also an example of grim humor — an ex- ample without a parallel in literature, so far as I know. Hamlet having killed Polonius is asked :

" Where's Polonius?"
" At supper."
" At supper ! where?"
" Not where he eats, but where he is eaten."

Above all others, Shakespeare appreciated the pathos of situation.

Nothing is more pathetic than the last scene in " Lear." No one has ever bent above his dead who did not feel the words uttered by the mad king, — words born of a despair deeper than tears :

> " Oh, that a horse, a dog, a rat hath life
> And thou no breath !"

So Iago, after he has been wounded, says :

> " I bleed, sir ; but not killed."

And Othello answers from the wreck and shattered remnant of his life :

> " I would have thee live ;
> For in my sense it is happiness to die."

When Troilus finds Cressida has been false, he cries :

> " Let it not be believed for womanhood ;
> Think ! we had mothers."

Ophelia, in her madness, " the sweet bells jangled out o' tune," says softly :

> " I would give you some violets ;
> But they withered all when my father died."

When Macbeth has reaped the harvest, the seeds of which were sown by his murderous hand, he exclaims,— and what could be more pitiful ?

> " I 'gin to be aweary of the sun."

Richard the Second feels how small a thing it is to be, or to have been, a king, or to receive honors

before or after power is lost ; and so, of those who
stood uncovered before him, he asks this piteous
question :

> " I live with bread, like you ; feel want,
> Taste grief, need friends ; subjected thus,
> How can you say to me I am a king ? "

Think of the salutation of Antony to the dead
Cæsar :

> " Pardon me, thou piece of bleeding earth."

When Pisanio informs Imogen that he had been
ordered by Posthumus to murder her, she bares her
neck and cries :

> " The lamb entreats the butcher :
> Where is thy knife ?   Thou art too slow
> To do thy master's bidding when I desire it."

Antony, as the last drops are falling from his self-
inflicted wound, utters with his dying breath to
Cleopatra, this :

> " I here importune death awhile, until
> Of many thousand kisses the poor last
> I lay upon thy lips."

To me, the last words of Hamlet are full of pathos :

> " I die, Horatio.
> The potent poison quite o'er crows my spirit * * *
> The rest is silence."

XVI.

SOME have insisted that Shakespeare must have been a physician, for the reason that he shows such knowledge of medicine — of the symptoms of disease and death—was so familiar with the brain, and with insanity in all its forms.

I do not think he was a physician. He knew too much—his generalizations were too splendid. He had none of the prejudices of that profession in his time. We might as well say that he was a musician, a composer, because we find in " The Two Gentlemen of Verona " nearly every musical term known in Shakespeare's time.

Others maintain that he was a lawyer, perfectly acquainted with the forms, with the expressions familiar to that profession — yet there is nothing to show that he was a lawyer, or that he knew more about law than any intelligent man should know.

He was not a lawyer. His sense of justice was never dulled by reading English law.

Some think that he was a botanist, because he named nearly all known plants. Others, that he was an astronomer, a naturalist, because he gave hints and suggestions of nearly all discoveries.

Some have thought that he must have been a
sailor, for the reason that the orders given in the
opening of " The Tempest " were the best that could,
under the circumstances, have been given to save
the ship.

For my part, I think there is nothing in the plays
to show that he was a lawyer, doctor, botanist or
scientist. He had the observant eyes that really
see, the ears that really hear, the brain that retains
all pictures, all thoughts, logic as unerring as light,
the imagination that supplies defects and builds the
perfect from a fragment. And these faculties, these.
aptitudes, working together, account for what he
did.

He exceeded all the sons of men in the splendor
of his imagination. To him the whole world paid
tribute, and nature poured her treasures at his feet.
In him all races lived again, and even those to be
were pictured in his brain.

He was a man of imagination — that is to say, of
genius, and having seen a leaf, and a drop of water,
he could construct the forests, the rivers, and the
seas — and in his presence all the cataracts would
fall and foam, the mists rise, the clouds form and
float.

If Shakespeare knew one fact, he knew its kindred
and its neighbors.   Looking at a coat of mail, he
instantly imagined the society, the conditions, that
produced it and what it, in turn, produced.   He saw
the castle, the moat, the draw-bridge, the lady in the
tower, and the knightly lover spurring across the
plain.   He saw the bold baron and the rude retainer,
the trampled serf, and all the glory and the grief of
feudal life.

He lived the life of all.

He was a citizen of Athens in the days of Pericles.
He listened to the eager eloquence of the great ora-
tors, and sat upon the cliffs, and with the tragic poet
heard "the multitudinous laughter of the sea."   He
saw Socrates thrust the spear of question through
the shield and heart of falsehood.   He was present
when the great man drank hemlock, and met the
night or death, tranquil as a star meets morning.
He listened to the peripatetic philosophers, and was
unpuzzled by the sophists.   He watched Phidias as
he chiseled shapeless stone to forms of love and
awe.

He lived by the mysterious Nile, amid the vast
and monstrous.   He knew the very thought that
wrought the form and features of the Sphinx.   He

heard great Memnon's morning song when marble
lips were smitten by the sun. He laid him down
with the embalmed and waiting dead, and felt within
their dust the expectation of another life, mingled
with cold and suffocating doubts — the children born
of long delay.

He walked the ways of mighty Rome, and saw
great Cæsar with his legions in the field. He stood
with vast and motley throngs and watched the
triumphs given to victorious men, followed by un-
crowned kings, the captured hosts, and all the spoils
of ruthless war. He heard the shout that shook the
Coliseum's roofless walls, when from the reeling
gladiator's hand the short sword fell, while from his
bosom gushed the stream of wasted life.

He lived the life of savage men. He trod the
forests' silent depths, and in the desperate game of
life or death he matched his thought against the instinct of the beast.

He knew all crimes and all regrets, all virtues and
their rich rewards. He was victim and victor, pur-
suer and pursued, outcast and king. He heard the
applause and curses of the world, and on his heart
had fallen all the nights and noons of failure and
success.

He knew the unspoken thoughts, the dumb desires, the wants and ways of beasts. He felt the crouching tiger's thrill, the terror of the ambushed prey, and with the eagles he had shared the ecstasy of flight and poise and swoop, and he had lain with sluggish serpents on the barren rocks uncoiling slowly in the heat of noon.

He sat beneath the bo-tree's contemplative shade, wrapped in Buddha's mighty thought, and dreamed all dreams that light, the alchemist, has wrought from dust and dew, and stored within the slumbrous poppy's subtle blood.

He knelt with awe and dread at every shrine — he offered every sacrifice, and every prayer — felt the consolation and the shuddering fear — mocked and worshipped all the gods — enjoyed all heavens, and felt the pangs of every hell.

. He lived all lives, and through his blood and brain there crept the shadow and the chill of every death, and his soul, like Mazeppa, was lashed naked to the wild horse of every fear and love and hate.

The Imagination had a stage in Shakespeare's brain, whereon were set all scenes that lie between the morn of laughter and the night of tears, and where his players bodied forth the false and true, the joys and griefs, the careless shallows and the tragic deeps of universal life.

From Shakespeare's brain there poured a Niagara of gems spanned by Fancy's seven-hued arch. He was as many-sided as clouds are many-formed. To him giving was hoarding — sowing was harvest — and waste itself the source of wealth. Within his marvellous mind were the fruits of all thought past, the seeds of all to be. As a drop of dew contains the image of the earth and sky, so all there is of life was mirrored forth in Shakespeare's brain.

Shakespeare was an intellectual ocean, whose waves touched all the shores of thought ; within which were all the tides and waves of destiny and will ; over which swept all the storms of fate, ambition and revenge ; upon which fell the gloom and darkness of despair and death and all the sunlight of content and love, and within which was the inverted sky lit with the eternal stars — an intellectual ocean — towards which all rivers ran, and from which now the isles and continents of thought receive their dew and rain.